Original title:
Treetop Tumbles

Copyright © 2025 Creative Arts Management OÜ
All rights reserved.

Author: Victor Mercer
ISBN HARDBACK: 978-1-80567-201-2
ISBN PAPERBACK: 978-1-80567-500-6

Reached by the Stars

In the heights where squirrels play,
A cat tries to jump in a silly way.
With a twist, a turn, and a little shout,
Down he goes, with a flurry of doubt.

A bird on a branch gives a noisy cheer,
As the cat tumbles down, without any fear.
Flapping and flailing, what a grand sight,
He lands in a pile of leaves, oh what a fright!

The chattering chipmunks giggle and squeal,
While the cat dusts off, giving them a heel.
Back to the climb, he must find his way,
But slick branches won't help him today!

With each wobble and stumble, a comedy show,
The tree seems to laugh, with a whispering glow.
Up he goes once more, with heart full of plans,
Though gravity waits with its mischievous hands!

Altitude Adventures

Up on high where squirrels play,
A flying acorn shot my way!
I ducked and rolled, it whizzed right by,
Such antics make me laugh and sigh.

With every leap, my balance sways,
In branches thick, my courage frays.
A misstep here, a bounce to there,
I'm off to join a nutty fair!

Windswept Wanderings

A gust so strong, I lost my cap,
It soared away, I'd expected that!
With tangled hair and goofy grin,
  I chase my hat as best I can.

The sky above, a canvas bright,
I swing and twirl, what a delight!
The clouds look down with twinkling eyes,
  While I perform my wild surprise.

Nestled in the Heights

My favorite nook is up a tree,
With mossy beds and views of glee.
A bird's complaint, a branch that bends,
Each day's a laugh, with silly friends.

I watch them gather twigs and leaves,
While plotting out their pranking thieves.
A birdie slips, oh what a sight!
He fluffed his feathers, took off in fright!

Enchanted Ascents

In climbs so high, we laugh and cheer,
As shadows stretch and daylight's near.
A leap of faith, a slide back down,
I'll wear the grass stains like a crown.

A surprise branch, it tickles my nose,
With giggles sparked as friendship grows.
We'll tumble down like acorns tossed,
In our laughter, we are never lost.

Nature's Breezy Waltz

The leaves all dance with glee,
A swirling, twirling spree.
Squirrels leap, a comic sight,
Chasing shadows, pure delight.

Branches sway in playful tune,
While bees hum a merry rune.
Laughter echoes from the sky,
As butterflies just zip on by.

Birds' Elysium

Chirps and tweets fill the air,
Feathered friends without a care.
In a flap, they twist and dive,
In the sky, they feel alive.

A group of finches takes a chance,
In mid-flight, they spin and dance.
Wings spread wide, a joyful blur,
Oh, what fun it is to stir!

Leafy Gymnastics

In high above, the branches sway,
A leaf performs, come what may.
With a flip and sudden twist,
It joins the breeze—oh, can't resist!

Laughter rings as acorns fall,
A misstep leads to leaps and rolls.
Nature's stage—what a grand view,
Where gymnasts wear a cloak of hue.

Aerial Antics

Two sparrows chase, in a playful race,
Around the oak, at a breakneck pace.
With a giggle, they spread their wings,
As hilarious chaos is what joy brings!

A starling slips, a little too bold,
Down it goes, with a comic fold.
Nature's antics—what a delight,
Where laughter echoes, day and night.

The Cradle of the Canopy

In branches high, a monkey swings,
His antics send the birds on flings.
A squirrel jokes with playful glee,
While leaves applaud his jubilee.

The sunlit stage, a leafy floor,
Each leap and bound reveals the lore.
With every twist, a laugh erupts,
As nature's whimsy interrupts.

Nature's Playground Above

A parrot slides on leafy slides,
With giggles echoing far and wide.
Bouncy vines like trampoline beds,
Where every critter holds their heads.

The raccoon joins, a queen of jest,
In acorn caps, she looks her best.
Squirrels pull pranks, no end in sight,
As laughter dances in the light.

Jumps Amongst the Treetops

A frog leaps high, in charming style,
His jumps could make the ground-mile smile.
With every splash, the river cheers,
As all the critters gather near.

A bear rolls down, his moves so slick,
While bees buzz round, don't miss a trick.
Together they frolic, try to slip,
In this wild world, no chance to trip.

Soaring Spirits

A kite-flying squirrel, bravely bold,
With winds of laughter, stories told.
Hiccups of joy from a nearby hare,
  As clouds above start to declare.

The sunbeams tickle, give a chase,
In nature's heart, find their place.
With every tumble, cheer resounds,
In this high realm where fun abounds.

Woodland Whimsy

In the branches, critters prance,
Squirrels twisting, take a chance.
Acorns falling, bounce and roll,
Nature giggles, feels the soul.

A raccoon slips, a curvy ride,
Down the bark, with playful pride.
Frogs leap high, they aim for stars,
Landing soft on passing cars!

Birds squawk loud in silly tunes,
Dancing under laughing moons.
Bumblebees in awkward flight,
Buzz around the maples bright.

When the sun begins to set,
The forest's laughs, you can't forget.
Whimsy dances in the air,
Joyful moments everywhere!

Adventures in the Arbor

High above the ground we soar,
Magic waits behind each door.
Chasing shadows, having fun,
Every branch, a new run!

Squirrels play their game of tag,
Swinging swift, they never lag.
Hiding nuts and laughing loud,
They're the jesters of the crowd.

A stork flies by, she spins around,
With every flap, she makes a sound.
Dropping snacks, the winds are wild,
Nature's antics, free and mild.

Through green leaves, we giggle pass,
Till we tumble, land with a splash!
Adventures call from high above,
It's a merry, playful love!

Aerial Musings

Between the boughs, the tales we find,
Whispered secrets, all entwined.
Monkeys swinging, oh so spry,
Always reaching for the sky.

Up so high, the view is grand,
While a raccoon takes a stand.
Peeking down at all below,
In this circus, putting on a show!

Leaves pirouette, like dancers bright,
Sun kisses branches, golden light.
A butterfly trips, stumbles too,
But shakes it off and flies anew.

With each twist, a chuckle shared,
In this realm, none are impaired.
Aerial dreams take off with glee,
In this forest, wild and free!

Up among the Leaves

In the treetops, laughter roams,
Skipping softly, finding homes.
Tangled branches, a playful race,
Frogs cheer on, their silly face.

Chirpy birds, they jest and tease,
Dodging squirrels with expert ease.
While chipmunks play their silly game,
In this wildwood, never tame.

Rustling leaves, they clap along,
A leafy choir sings its song.
Butterflies flit, a slapstick show,
Tickled petals sway to and fro.

As stars peek through the leafy shroud,
Nature giggles, and we feel proud.
Living life in careless splendor,
Up where joy is a daily lender!

Hovering Over Dreams

In the branches, squirrels prance,
As acorns dance their silly chance.
A bird with flair, wears a tiny hat,
Sings tales of nuts, and where they're at.

A breeze that tickles through the leaves,
Whispers laughter, and gently weaves.
With every flutter from up above,
They gather round, in giggles of love.

Melody in the Meadow's Midst

Bumblebees buzz like they've found a tune,
While grasshoppers hop under the moon.
A rabbit jigs, while the daisies sway,
In this meadow, who needs ballet?

The flowers sway in a vibrant show,
With petals that clap, row by row.
Even the frogs join the merry spree,
Croaking echoes of wild glee.

Whirling in the Wind

Leaves twirl around in a whirly dance,
As breezes catch them in a playful trance.
A feisty gust sweeps a hat away,
Spinning it off like a child at play.

The trees lean in with mirthful cheer,
Sharing secrets only they hear.
With every gust, laughter takes flight,
A whimsical game from day until night.

Ascending Echoes

Up high where the sunbeams tickle the sky,
A raccoon in shades gives a wink and a sigh.
Chasing his tail, he leaps with glee,
He might just think he's a bird, you see.

With each leap, he stirs up a storm,
As clouds chuckle at his acrobatic form.
"Sweet heights!" he shouts to the blue above,
In the tree tops, he finds his spot of love.

The Height of Day

In the branches high and wide,
A squirrel wears a comical stride.
With acorns packed on every side,
He spins and twirls in joyful pride.

The sun shines bright, a funny sight,
As birds engage in silly flight.
They chase their tails with pure delight,
While ants have parties in the light.

Spiraling Leaves and Soaring Hearts

Leaves take a leap in whirling dance,
While children giggle, seizing chance.
They spin and twirl, lost in their glance,
    As laughter twitters in a trance.

A puppy jumps, a kite takes fling,
    In the treetops, joy's a king.
With every gust, more smiles do bring,
    As nature hums, and songbirds sing.

Adventures Above the World

Up above where the wild things play,
A monkey swings and steals the day.
He pulls a prank in a cheeky way,
Then laughs it off and dashes away.

With each new branch, surprises bloom,
Rescue missions from a forest tomb.
They tumble down, a leafy plume,
Creating smiles, dispelling gloom.

Boughs and Boundaries

Between the leaves, a raccoon peeks,
Plotting mischief, oh, how it sneaks!
With antics bold, it plays hide-and-seek,
While chattering birds share their critiques.

Underneath the boughs, tales unfold,
Where dreams are sung and laughter's bold.
Adventures bloom in hearts of gold,
In a world where joy is never sold.

Summit Serenade

Atop the branches, squirrels prance,
They dance and twirl, take quite a chance.
With acorns gliding, laughter rings,
Even the birds join in on these flings.

A cat below plots a pounce,
But finds it hard to make a bounce.
The treetop crew gives a hearty cheer,
As they swing and sway without any fear.

Breezy Balancing Acts

A raccoon struts on a slender twig,
Wobbling sideways, oh, what a gig!
Fell off once, but up he goes,
Chasing the wind, how clumsily he flows!

The chattering magpies shout and jeer,
With flapping wings, they lend an ear.
A feathered friend takes to the skies,
While giggling low, the gang complicates their tries.

Overhead Adventures

Boosted high by a zephyr's spree,
A playful puppy climbs a tree.
Barking at clouds, chasing the sun,
What a whirlwind of frolic and fun!

He tumbles through leaves, a furry sight,
While critters giggle at his wild flight.
Up above, the branches sway,
In this zany world, they play all day.

Lively Leaves

Leaves to the left, then whirls away,
A hungry chipmunk joins the fray.
Bounding through branches, he skips with glee,
Diving for snacks, what a sight to see!

A dance-off begins with a cheeky crow,
He shakes his tail and puts on a show.
The forest giggles at the ruckus and cheer,
Who knew such fun could sprout from mere air?

Skyward Journeys

Squirrels racing up the trunk,
Wings of bluebirds, all a-bunk.
Down they tumble, no soft land,
Chasing acorns like it's grand.

Branches sway and giggles flow,
Playful dances, head to toe.
Laughter echoes, quite absurd,
Nature's stage, each twist a word.

Fluttering Foliage

Leaves like hats on tiny heads,
Flapping wings where mischief spreads.
Underneath, a party stirs,
As critters sing and spin like blurs.

A ladybug takes center stage,
With a grasshopper, in a rage.
Jumping high, they form a whirl,
Dizzy dancers, what a twirl!

Secrets of the Upper World

High above where whispers play,
Gossip travels, light and gay.
Chirps and chirrups, all around,
What's that secret? Lost and found!

A serving of the sunlit pie,
While bumblebees dance and fly.
Despite their size, they dare to boast,
Claiming pollen like a roast!

Breezy Escapades

Pinecones tumble, what a sight!
An acorn rolls, oh what delight!
Windy pranks of nature's hand,
   Encouraging a merry band.

Perched on branches, birds conspire,
To send a sneeze, oh, what a fire!
Down the hill, they shake and slide,
In this game, there's no place to hide.

Songs from the Summit

High above, the squirrels prance,
They throw acorns in a dance.
A bird sings out with goofy flair,
While branches sway without a care.

Monkeys tumble, slip, and slide,
In the leaves, they try to hide.
Their giggles echo through the air,
As they swing without a worry or a scare.

A raccoon joins with silly glee,
In his paws, a cup of tea.
He spills it all, oh what a sight,
Laughing as he falls from height.

So come and share a laugh with me,
In the treetops, wild and free.
Where nature's pranks are always near,
And every climb brings joyful cheer.

The Secret Life Above

Whispers among the leafy boughs,
The secrets kept by furry pals.
A sloth snores loud, what a delight,
While owls wink in the soft moonlight.

Acorns tumble with a plop,
Squirrel's snack—he'll never stop.
Each critter thinks they're in a dream,
As they plot their next big scheme.

Parrots squawk with crazy chatter,
Bouncing where the branches scatter.
A game of tag? They're all a-flutter,
With every leap, the leaves just shudder.

So listen close, and you may hear,
The laughter shared without a fear.
In this world that's up high and free,
Joy scampers on each twirling tree.

Treescapes of Thrill

Bouncing vines and leafy swings,
Nature hides its funny things.
A chipmunk stumbles, oh, what fun,
As sunlight dances, brighter than the sun.

With every twist and every slide,
The woodpecker joins in with pride.
He taps a tune, a quirky beat,
All while perched on a branch's seat.

Jumpy frogs leap from stem to stem,
Clumsily, they're a silly gem.
They croak a song, but oh so wrong,
Yet somehow it all seems to belong.

In the foliage, laughter rings,
Nature's antics send us in swings.
High above, where fun's the aim,
We'll cheer for all in this funny game.

Skyward Bound

Up, up high, the world's a hoot,
Where every animal wears a suit.
The fox in shades, the bear in boots,
No tree is safe from their cute pursuits.

Tree frogs leap with style and flair,
While the raccoon steals a snazzy chair.
They all convene for games of tag,
While squirrels zap like a racing flag.

The breeze carries laughter and glee,
As each creature climbs joyfully.
Embrace the fun with every bound,
In this wild, uproarious playground.

So if you hear a giggle or squawk,
Join the fun on this leafy walk.
In nature's playground, bright and warm,
Expect the laughs to always swarm.

Fables of the Forest Canopy

A squirrel with dreams so grand,
Decided to start a rock band.
With acorns for drums, and leaves for strings,
He called all the critters to join in and sing.

The owls hooted out the beat,
While rabbits danced on their tiny feet.
Through branches they swayed, oh what a show,
Even the tired old trees started to glow.

A fox brought his flute, quite refined,
And claimed he could solo and blow their minds.
But each time he played, the notes flew away,
Leaving him grumpy and slightly dismayed.

Yet as the sun dipped low in the sky,
They laughed till their bellies would surely cry.
In the canopy, legends were spun, you see,
Of that wild woodland concert, as fun as can be.

Heights of Imagination

A bird with a cap and sunglasses on,
Claimed he could see the whole world from dawn.
Climbing up trees, he waved to a bee,
"Isn't life grand? Come dance here with me!"

The bee buzzed around, unsure of the play,
Said, "I'm just busy, but hey, maybe later today!"
They made quite a scene, the bird and his friend,
Creating a ruckus that would never end.

A raccoon strolled by, with a grape on his head,
"Why wear fruits, dear bird? Here's a joke instead!"
With laughter and jokes, they spun 'round and spun,
In their high-flying world where the fun's never done.

Each branch held their giggles, oh what a sight,
With dreams that soared high into the night.
Imagination sparked, and laughter took flight,
In their raucous little world, everything felt right.

Above the Ground

In the treetops where antics unfold,
Lived a young turtle, quite brave and bold.
He climbed a tall branch, his heart filled with glee,
Said, "Look at me! I can fly, don't you see?"

A cat up above, resplendent in fur,
Challenged him softly with a casual purr.
"Flying's for birds, my dear turtley friend,
But you sure aim high, it's a good way to spend!"

The turtle replied, "I'll invent something new,
A way to flip, dance, and glide like you!"
With a twirl and a spin, all the squirrels did cheer,
At the sight of such courage and laughter so clear.

So up in the branches, they played without care,
Inventing wild games, tossing worries in air.
In a world off the ground, where imagination swirls,
A turtle can fly, and joy unravels and twirls.

Floating with the Fronds

A leaf let go with a soft little flap,
Danced with the wind, what a whimsical tap.
It giggled and whirled as it tumbled around,
In a whimsical game on the playground of ground.

A chameleon watched from his branch up high,
Declared, "I can change colors, just watch me try!"
He shifted through hues, a dazzling display,
While the leaf chuckled softly, "You're bright, I'll say!"

Suddenly, a frog hopped up with a grin,
Said, "On a leaf I would love to begin!"
So they spun in mid-air, a trio of dare,
Creating a ruckus with laughter to share.

With ferns and fronds all around in delight,
The critters joined in, oh, what a sight!
In the limbs of the trees, where silliness thrives,
They floated through fun, feeling oh so alive!

Climbing for Joy

I scaled a bough with a laugh,
My hat flew off in a daft path.
The squirrels cheered for my big leap,
While below, my friends just couldn't peep.

A monkey swung by with a grin,
Hollering, "Come join the fun, jump in!"
But I tripped over my shoelace tight,
And tumbled down—oh, what a sight!

The branches danced as I fell,
Every thud sounded like a bell.
My socks were green, my face was red,
I left with laughter, not with dread.

So up I go, without a care,
With each wild swing, I brush the air.
For every tumble, there's a cheer,
In the canopy, joy is near!

Chasing the Clouds

I ran to catch a cloud so bright,
With puffs of fluff, oh what a sight!
I leaped up high and missed the mark,
Landed on a branch with a spark.

The breeze gave chase, a playful race,
I spun around, what a clumsy grace!
A parrot rolled his eyes at me,
Said, "You won't catch what you can't see!"

With gratitude, I took a pause,
To laugh out loud at nature's laws.
The sky can giggle, and so shall I,
As I wave to passing birds up high!

So if you hear a thud and clap,
Just know I'm in a cloud-chasing flap.
With laughter trailing behind me fast,
I'll keep on playing, my joy steadfast!

Canopy Connections

Up in the branches, a chatty crew,
A raccoon, a gecko, and a wise old ewe.
They shared their tales of daring feats,
While munching on some berry treats.

The raccoon chimed, "Let's start a band!"
"On leafy branches, isn't it grand?"
The gecko croaked a silly tune,
That echoed 'neath the smiling moon.

I joined the fun with my best dance move,
With every twirl, my troubles do lose.
Caught on a vine, I spun with flair,
A brief mishap, but who would care?

In this high world, we share our jokes,
From fluttering leaves to laughing folks.
So when you find a tangled vine,
Remember the laughter we entwine!

Roaming the Ribbons of Leaf

Among the leaves, I weave my way,
A tapestry bright where memories play.
Each step I take, I giggle and sway,
For nature's whispers have much to say.

I bumped a wallaby, oh what a clout,
He dashed away, without a doubt.
"Excuse my flailing!" I called with glee,
As he hopped away, still laughing at me.

In the dance of branches, I twirled and spun,
Caught a glimpse of the moon, oh what fun!
With playful rustling under my feet,
Every leaf a friend, every sound a treat.

So here I roam on this leafy stage,
Laughter the script, joy my wage.
From high above to the floor below,
In this leafy realm, my silliness flows!

Feathers and Foliage

A squirrel in a bow tie, oh what a sight,
Dancing on branches with all of his might.
He twirls and he flips, with vigor he bounds,
Chasing his shadow, lost in the sounds.

A bird joins the party, singing off-key,
Flapping his wings, so wild and free.
Together they tumble, a hilarious game,
With nuts as confetti, who is to blame?

The leaves shake with laughter, swaying so low,
As critters all gather, in line for the show.
They giggle and wiggle, a sight to behold,
In this leafy circus, their stories unfold.

So raise up your glasses, toast to the cheer,
To friendships in branches, and laughter sincere.
In nature's grand stage, all worries dissolve,
In this whimsical world, we all shall evolve.

Gala of the Greenery

Among the tall trees, a dance has begun,
Where leaves sway to rhythms, oh what fun!
A turtle with parties, a waddle so spry,
Makes guests laugh hard, as they watch him try.

A bevy of bugs, in bright little suits,
Tap dances on petals, oh how it hoots!
They spin and they swirl, under sun's warm ray,
Creating a ruckus, leading the way.

A raccoon with charm, wearing a hat,
Whispers of secrets while stealing a snack.
With berries and nuts piled high on his plate,
He's quite the showman, oh isn't that great?

At twilight, they gather, beneath the wide sky,
With laughter and stories, oh how time flies!
In this gala of green, where joy knows no end,
Nature's own ballroom, where all hearts mend.

Up and Away with Nature

An acorn took flight, with a gust of the breeze,
   Spinning and twirling, oh what a tease!
With squirrels as pilots, they zigzag and zoom,
   Creating a whirlwind, a leaf-covered room.

A raccoon in goggles screams 'Look at me!'
   As he takes to the air, quite wild and free.
With his snacks flying high, he giggles aloud,
   As flowers erupt, cheering for the crowd.

The clouds burst with laughter, as they float on by,
   Watching the antics, they whisper a sigh.
From twig to the heavens, all critters unite,
   In a wacky parade, a marvelous flight.

When finally down to the ground they descend,
With leaves in their hair, they'll boast to their friends.
   In the forest's embrace, they'll recount the tale,
   Of courage and chaos, a whimsical sail.

Ribbons of Green

Twirling like ribbons, the vines swing around,
A raccoon on a vine, upside down he's found.
The leaves join the party, swaying with glee,
   As they tickle the nose of a nearby bee.

A parade of critters, each more absurd,
A frog plays a flute, quite clever, preferred.
With splashes of laughter, and hiccups in time,
   Nature's got rhythm, a fun little rhyme.

Giggling branches, with stories to share,
   As a gust of cool air tousles their hair.
They dance in the moonlight, a sight quite pathetic,
   Yet charmingly awkward, and oh so kinetic!

A toast to the forest, where silliness reigns,
   With critters and leaves, and delightful refrains.
In ribbons of green, joy dances with grace,
   In this comedy haven, we all find our place.

Skylines and Silhouettes

Up in the air, a squirrel leaps high,
Chasing a feather that dances on by.
He twirls and he spins with exuberant glee,
Hoping the wind will set him free.

A pigeon looked on, with raised eyebrows,
Wondering what on earth is this about.
The acorn above, it shakes and it rolls,
As laughter erupts from the treetop souls.

A branch makes a crack and everyone squeals,
It's a wild rollercoaster, no seatbelts or wheels.
Birds cheer him on, hooting with joy,
Cheered by the antics of their furry boy.

With every wild tumble, the day turns to night,
As critters take flight, in sheer delight.
They caper and cavort, it's a silly affair,
Every tumble and tumble is met with a stare!

Flight of Fancy

A raccoon sets sail on a leaf boat so wide,
With a wobbly journey and paws open wide.
He tips to one side, and the water's a splash,
A cascade of giggles, as he makes a crash.

A chatter of monkeys, they swing overhead,
With a giggle and glance, they do what they're fed.
A leap and a flip, then a swing on a vine,
Graceful, they say, but they stumble like swine!

An owl feigns wisdom, looks down with a sigh,
How do they manage to fly by like that guy?
A laugh and a wink, he sips tea from a cup,
Wonders if squirrels can actually give up.

With feathers and fur, they create quite a scene,
In a carnival hustle, all joyous and keen.
At dusk they unite, their tales to recount,
Of the fumbles and flails, they swear it's no count!

Beneath the Canopy

Squirrels collide, it's a comedy show,
As one takes a leap, he lands just below.
With a puff and a hoot, they roll in the leaves,
Cackling and squeaking as nature retrieves.

A fox wanders in with a slight little trot,
Seeing the tumble, he gives it a shot.
But his paw gets stuck in a twig's little snare,
He blinks at the bushes, is anyone there?

A bunny hops in with a sense of pure cheer,
His ears bobbing high, he can't see the near.
With a twitch and a jump, he gets tangled in vines,
A fiesta of fumbles in nature's designs.

Yet laughter erupts, like echoes in air,
A symphony of giggles this day has to share.
With every odd tumble, they gather and play,
Creating a ruckus until the end of the day!

Heights of Wonder

A cat on a branch thinks she's a grand queen,
Overseeing her realm, all fluffy and clean.
But a gust of wind offers a twisty surprise,
Off she goes tumbling, oh, how she flies!

Down comes a possum with mischief in mind,
He sees her descent, oh the fun he can find!
With a grin on his face, he joins in the spree,
Comically tumbling, as wild as can be.

Under the shadows, a bear hears the ruckus,
Decides to join in, brings snacks in his focus.
But balance he lacks, and he trips on a nut,
Rolls down the slope, oh dear, what a rut!

The crowd's in a frenzy, they cheer for the show,
Like a circus ensues under skies high and low.
With every hilarious fall, it brings such delight,
As critters all giggle till the last of the light!

Leafy Leaps

A squirrel with a joyful flare,
Takes the plunge, floats through the air.
With acorns clutched in tiny paws,
He lands with style, earning applause.

A hop, a skip, then a tumble down,
Spinning like a merry clown.
A leaf that twirls just like a toy,
His forest friends all shout with joy.

He flips through branches, around each bend,
Creating chaos, but it's a trend!
With every bounce, there's laughter loud,
Oh, the antics of this cheeky crowd!

So here's to leaps both wild and free,
Nature's jesters, a sight to see.
For every splash and silly dive,
Brings forth smiles, oh, what a vibe!

Skyward Serenades

In tallest trees where whispers play,
A robin sings the funniest way.
His notes are quirky, off the beat,
Bouncing like a child on two small feet.

A cat up high tries to sing along,
But with each note, it purrs, then throngs.
The leaves all rustle with great cheer,
Together they dance, no hint of fear.

A breeze comes by, shaking the air,
Branching out with a wild flair.
Creating giggles from down below,
As squirrels spin in a tangled show.

So let the skies be filled with fun,
As feathered friends outshine the sun.
Through melodies that flip and swoop,
Join in the laughter, come, let's loop!

The Dance of the Dappled Shadows

In sunlight's glow, shadows prance,
Branches sway, and leaves take a chance.
A lizard joins in the frolic, too,
With moves so funky, who knew he could do?

Mice twirl 'round in a joyful chase,
Making the most of this lively space.
With every leap and tiny spin,
Leaves giggle softly, letting fun in.

A chipmunk DJ spins a beat,
As the woodland crowd begins to greet.
The disco lights of dappled green,
Make every creature feel like a queen!

So twirl in place, with glee so bright,
Let shadows dance through day and night.
For in this grove, laughter does soar,
Happiness blooms forevermore!

Up High Adventures

A squirrel's calling, "Let's take flight!"
With stunts so bold, they're quite the sight.
They bound through treetops, twist and twirl,
An acrobatic show causes hearts to whirl.

There's a parrot squawking jokes up high,
As butterflies flutter and a badger sighs.
"Why did the tree refuse to sway?"
"Too stiff to dance, it chooses to stay!"

With leaps so grand and flips so neat,
Nuts become balls in this backyard feat.
The laughter echoes through the blue,
As furry friends just love to strew.

So let's join in, up high we'll go,
Where fun and folly put on a show.
For every tumble, let's cheer and shout,
In these branches, joy's what it's about!

Swaying in the Breeze

Leaves waltz round with glee,
Branches bend and sway,
A squirrel doing acrobatics,
   In joy it leaps and plays.

A crow drops crumbs from high,
While chipmunks chase with haste,
Bouncing off the bark, they fly,
   With laughter held in taste.

Breezes giggle through the trees,
Their whispers full of cheer,
As nature's jesters do as they please,
   It's a feast of fun right here.

Up they go, with careless grace,
Caught in a twist and spin,
Under moonlight's gentle face,
   Their night of joy begins.

Ascending Dreams

High above the bustling ground,
A ruckus starts to rise,
Where daring dreams can be found,
Underneath the open skies.

A bear tries to climb a vine,
With moves both wild and bold,
The branches jibe and say, "Divine!"
As gravity's grip takes hold.

Parrots squawk in vibrant hues,
While squirrels tumble down,
They dance away the morning blues,
In their leafy, lofty crown.

Who knew heights could be this fun?
With giggles and a cheer,
In dreams of mischief brightly spun,
Our laughter draws them near.

Nature's Highwire

A raccoon walks on a limb,
Juggling snacks with flair,
The crowd below begins to whim,
As acorns dance in air.

A fox slips, almost takes a dive,
Bouncing back, it sprawls,
With the spirit of the tree alive,
Its laughter often calls.

Nuts and leaves, a jester's stage,
With critters stealing shows,
Each twist and turn, a lively page,
Where silly mischief grows.

High above the yawning crowd,
Life's antics brightly gleam,
And on this line, both bold and proud,
They share their comic dream.

A Flutter Amongst the Foliage

A butterfly takes flight today,
Twisting and twirling free,
While bouncing buds and blooms at play,
Join in a leafy spree.

Bees in hats do dance a jig,
Pollen dust in the air,
With every hop, each jump, each gig,
Nature's humor laid bare.

Leaves laugh softly in the breeze,
As squirrels chase their tails,
In this garden full of ease,
They weave their epic trails.

Joyful leaps and silly spins,
Among the greens they hum,
In every flitter, joy begins,
A chorus loud and fun.

Skyward Somersaults

Squirrels leap from branch to branch,
With acorn dreams and daring plans.
They twist and flip in vivid dance,
While birds above just shake their fans.

A bumblebee buzzes by in haste,
As leaves do cartwheels to the ground.
Each gust a joke, a merry taste,
Nature giggles, full of sound.

Raccoons in masks make quite the scene,
Doing backflips off the trees.
Their antics spark a comical sheen,
As laughter rides on playful breeze.

Oh, the canopy filled with cheer,
Where every tumble earns a smile.
Joy and chuckles linger here,
Making each leap quite worthwhile.

Whispering Winds

Leaves chatter softly in the air,
As branches sway with pure delight.
The rustling whispers, full of flair,
Encourage critters to take flight.

Chipmunks juggle seeds in glee,
While frogs observe from low to high.
With little hops and bounces free,
They join the fun beneath the sky.

A cat with flair sits on a sway,
Contemplating each plucky jump.
Will tails get tangled? Oh, hooray!
As giggles rise, they thump and thump.

Nature's giggle fills the trees,
With stories spun in every gust.
The world is light, flush with the tease,
Where every leap ignites our trust.

Ascending Acrobatics

Monkeys swing in grand ballet,
Their laughter echoes through the air.
With silly flips they love to play,
They turn the woods into a fair.

Each vine's a swing, each trunk a dive,
As they defy the laws of gravity.
With every twist, they seem alive,
Creating chaos, oh so savvy!

Parrots squawk, they're quite the crowd,
Cheering leaps through leafy lanes.
Their colors bright, they're loud and proud,
Adding to all the playful strains.

Look, there goes a squirrel on a ride,
And balance beams made out of bark.
Through ups and downs, they're filled with pride,
In the treetops, let's embark!

Dancing in the Canopy

A jolly troupe on branches dance,
With twirls and spins full of mirth.
The leaves join in this leafy trance,
   A merry fest upon the earth.

With every jump, they toast the sun,
While shadows play upon the grass.
It's truly a wild, joyful run,
Where time turns slow, and giggles pass.

Crickets chirp a happy tune,
As creatures prance with boundless zest.
Underneath the bright full moon,
Each twirl a treasure, a light jest.

So come and join this leafy spree,
Where laughter dances on the breeze.
In nature's arms, we live carefree,
   A party held among the trees.

Foliage Frolic

Leaves giggle in the breeze,
Squirrels jump with such great ease.
Branches twist like silly straws,
While chipmunks dance without a pause.

A raccoon wears a leaf as a hat,
He shimmies too, imagine that!
Pinecones fall like rubber balls,
As laughter echoes through the halls.

A dizzy owl spins 'round and round,
Chasing shadows on the ground.
The forest floor, a comical stage,
Where every critter turns a page.

Sunlight spills, a golden shower,
Making butterflies dance with power.
In this laughing canopy high,
Foliage frolics catch the eye.

Glimpse of the Sky

A parrot yells, 'Hey, look up there!'
He's caught a cloud, a fluffy share.
Ducks play tag in a bright blue dome,
As bumblebees buzz far from home.

An airplane's just a bigger bird,
The trees below laugh out loud, unheard.
They're waving their arms, saying, 'We're fine!'
While critters in seats try to recline.

A cactus spy in the desert gaze,
Winks at passersby in a funny craze.
The sun takes selfies, showing its grin,
As the moon peeks out, ready to join in.

With giggles of air, clouds do a dance,
Sunbeams step out for a sunny prance.
In this wild sky, where silliness flies,
Laughter echoes as high as the eyes.

Celestial Capers

Stars toss glitter like confetti,
While moons bounce low, all bright and petty.
Galaxies swirl in a dancing tease,
Tickling space with cosmic ease.

A comet plays hide and seek,
As crickets chirp, their music squeaks.
Constellations giggle, rearranging their map,
While a dandelion dreams of its next nap.

Planets spin on a merry-go-round,
While asteroids jump like they're spellbound.
The Milky Way pours laughter in streams,
As even the void giggles in dreams.

Time takes a leap through a starlit trap,
Making each moment a blissful clap.
In the cosmic circus, so much to share,
Each celestial caper hangs in the air.

Woodland Wanderlust

A hedgehog rolls with endless zeal,
Finding treasures, oh what a deal!
Bamboo whispers secrets to the breeze,
While raccoons giggle beneath tall trees.

Footprints lead to mischief galore,
Dancing through the forest floor.
Frogs hop high for a tree-top view,
Jumping with joy, oh how they flew!

Mushrooms laugh as the rain rolls by,
While squirrels leap to touch the sky.
A butterfly flutters with flamboyant flair,
Telling tales of its travels through the air.

Every leaf is a giggling friend,
Joining in the mirth without end.
In this woodland, where wanderlust blooms,
Nature thrives and joyingly consumes.

Canopy Whispers

In leafy halls where squirrels prance,
They tell their tales of clumsy dance.
A branch too low, a leap too wide,
One fluffy tail, and off they glide.

They giggle softly in the breeze,
While juggling acorns with such ease.
A slip, a trip, and down they flop,
The sound of laughter never stops.

With each playful twist and turn,
The secret joys of life we learn.
A peek-a-boo behind the bark,
Life's little pranks, they leave a mark.

So when you stroll beneath the green,
Look up for shows that can't be seen.
A world of giggles high above,
In branches swaying, laughter's love.

Fluttering Leaves

A leaf took off, a daring flight,
It wrapped a squirrel in sheer delight.
They twirled and whirled in dizzy glee,
The funniest sight, oh can't you see?

Around and around, they spun so fast,
A comedy act that couldn't last.
They tumbled down, a fuzzy pair,
Through branches thick, into the air.

A bird laughed loud, a chirpy tease,
As they got stuck up in the trees.
But with a wiggle and a twist,
They freed themselves, and yet they missed.

The ground below, oh what a trip,
Landed soft on a mushroom tip.
With wobbly legs, they stood up straight,
And chased more fun, oh isn't fate great?

Heights of Laughter

In skies so high, the critters play,
Chasing sunshine through the day.
They flip and flop, those furry friends,
With giggles echoing, fun never ends.

A raccoon slipped on a slicky vine,
While laughing hard, it felt divine.
The branches shook with each good laugh,
As critters shared their silly path.

A woodpecker's joke fell from a tree,
"Knock knock!" it cried, "Who's it gonna be?"
But down below, a cat did spy,
And into the leaves, the jokes would fly.

With every fall and joyful cheer,
Up in the heights, there's nothing to fear.
Laughter dances on the breeze,
In nature's stage, life's wild tease.

Branches' Play

Oh what a game the branches make,
They twist and jiggle for fun's own sake.
With every leap, a hearty crash,
A falling acorn, and then a splash.

Back and forth, the tails do swing,
Nature's jesters, they laugh and sing.
Branches bow with playful grace,
As laughter paints a silly face.

A daring jump from twig to twig,
One branch too far, and down goes Pig!
But giggles rise and fill the air,
As friends all gather 'round to care.

With every tumble, joy they find,
In tangled limbs, their hearts entwined.
Let's dance with nature's merry crew,
In branches' play, we all renew.

Swaying Silhouettes

In the breeze, a dance begins,
Branches wiggle, leaves wear grins.
Squirrels bounce from limb to limb,
Chasing shadows, their lights dim.

A wobbly bird, quite out of tune,
Sings of hiccups under the moon.
With flapping wings that twist and slide,
On a branch, it's quite the ride.

A raccoon giggles, holding tight,
To a swinging vine, a silly sight.
He tumbles down with a playful squeak,
And lands right where the owls peek.

The sun dips low, the shadows stretch,
Nature laughs, no need to fetch.
With each sway and goofy glide,
The forest thrives, and joys collide.

Playful Perches

A chubby hippo on a twig,
Claims it's spry, what a big gig!
With an ounce of spark as it sways,
It hums a tune for the sunny days.

Three blue jays plot a funny prank,
Spilling berries down the plank.
Splat! They roll and laugh aloud,
As they dive into the goofy crowd.

An awkward frog leaps way too far,
Landing in style, a bright green star.
In leaps and bounds, it won't retreat,
Transforming branches into a feat.

With joyous squeals and laughter true,
The vibrant leaves dance, a wild crew.
Each branch a stage, in perfect tune,
As dusk arrives beneath the moon.

Upside-Down Horizons

Hang a squirrel, upside down,
With a nutty grin, our woodland clown.
He spins and twirls in dizzy glee,
While giggling critters watch with glee.

A straying raccoon finds a nest,
To take a nap? Oh, what a jest!
He snores a tune that splits the air,
While gingerly perched without a care.

Nuts fly high with a cheerful clunk,
As the crow comes next, a sneaky punk.
But with a swift and clumsy dive,
The case of nutty grace, contrived.

Through giggles and snickers, the forest hums,
With all its charm, the laughter comes.
In the wild, where fun abounds,
Upside-down, the joy surrounds.

Gravity's Gentle Embrace

When branches bend beneath the cheer,
Gravity smiles and draws us near.
A fluttering leaf, with laughter flies,
Dancing down to the soft surprise.

A bouncy squirrel leaps with ease,
Clutching twigs like acrobatic bees.
With every twist and silly dive,
He chuckles loud, oh, how he thrives!

A parrot squawks, it's time to play,
Riding the wind in a feathered sway.
With ticklish tails and tickled feet,
The wild is grand, oh, what a treat!

As dusk arrives, the fun won't cease,
With chuckles shared, a shared peace.
In this playful world, hold tight the lace,
As we tumble down in gravity's embrace.

Echoes in the Alder

A squirrel jumped high, did a twist,
He landed on branches, gave a list.
"I'm the king of this tree, can't you see?"
And laughed at the leaves, so wild and free.

The woodpecker knocked, 'Come out, take a ride!'
On a big bouncy leaf where the acorn hides.
A dancing chipmunk joined in the fun,
Spinning in circles, oh what a run!

They giggled and squeaked as branches would sway,
In the shade of the sun, they laughed all day.
A raccoon peeked in, just to join the spree,
But fell in a bush, now covered in leaves!

The echoes of laughter rang through the glade,
As nature's mischief in sunlight played.
With snacks in their paws and jobs on a break,
This meeting of critters, oh what a mistake!

Canopy Capers

Up in the boughs, a party did start,
With acorns as hats and laughs from the heart.
The branches did sway, they danced in delight,
A parade of the weird, oh what a sight!

A parrot flew in, with a joke of a pun,
"Why did the worm think it was done?"
It wriggled and jiggled, adding some flair,
As laughter erupted, filling the air.

The owls were wise, with their serious traits,
But even they snickered, ignoring debates.
Chasing their tails, a young fox took a leap,
And fell in a bush, landing in a heap!

Mischief and mayhem danced underneath leaves,
Squirrels a-chatter in hilarious weave.
From whispers of humor, the laughter takes flight,
In this quirky tree world, all feels just right!

Branching Out

One day a frog took a jump from the ground,
Said, "I'll be a bird, let's see what I've found!"
He leaped to a branch, feeling quite proud,
Till he slipped on a leaf, fell right through the crowd.

Squirrels exclaimed with a raucous cheer,
"Next time, dear friend, stay close to the sphere!"
But the frog only winked and gave a good grin,
"I'll try it again; let the fun now begin!"

The raccoon's costume of feathers so bright,
Made all of them giggle, a comical sight.
With laughter like thunder echoing along,
This tree of odd creatures sang a silly song.

So if you look up from where you stand tall,
You'll see the adventures of critters, and all.
In branches, they tumble with giggles around,
Creating a ruckus, pure joy can be found!

Whispers of the Wind

In the breeze, leaves fluttered with glee,
As a gopher popped up saying, "Look at me!"
He juggled some nuts, all while on a vine,
Oops, there goes the acorn, rolling on time!

A turtle arrived in a cowboy hat high,
"I'm in it to win it!" he shouted to the sky.
As the winds held their breath in a quizzical hush,
The turtle's quick strut turned into a rush!

Branches were bending from laughter and sound,
With antics afoot, so much joy to be found.
A hedgehog rolled in with a dance to display,
Spinning, he slipped, and rolled far away!

In shadows and sunlight, the fun never ends,
For silliness here makes the best of friends.
So listen closely to whispers so sly,
Where mischief meets laughter, watch the fun fly!

Arboreal Jests

Squirrels in shorts, they take a leap,
Chasing acorns, not a care, not a peep.
Branches wobble, donuts they spin,
A feathery ballet, let the laughter begin.

Goats with sunglasses, strutting their stuff,
Nimbly they balance; is that enough?
Frogs in a chorus, singing their song,
Adventures in branches, where things can go wrong.

Birds with bow ties, they dance in a row,
Shrugging off falls, they steal the show.
Nests made of googly eyes and string,
In this leafy circus, joy is the king.

And at day's end, as shadows grow long,
The giggling leaves join the animal throng.
With a hop and a flap, they tumble and dive,
In this tree-top world, oh how we thrive!

High Above the Earth

A raccoon on stilts, oh what a sight,
Balancing fruit, what a daring flight!
With a plonk and a flop, he lands with a grin,
In this leafy realm, let the fun begin!

Macaws in a marching band leading the way,
Flapping and flailing, come watch them sway.
What's that on the branch? A pie, oh so round,
As it tumbles down, laughter's the sound.

A hedgehog in shades, rolling downhill,
Tripping on twigs, now that's quite a thrill!
Pinecones as projectiles, shot from a slingshot,
In this frolicsome tree, there's mischief a lot.

Perched high above, with roots intertwining,
Creatures abound, the fun is aligning.
Each turn, each spring, with giggles they share,
Life in the canopy is beyond compare!

Vertiginous Escapades

Kites made of leaves soaring high and wide,
Chasing the wind, they whimsically glide.
A beetle in boots, navigating the climb,
In this vaudeville stunt, everything's fine!

Dancing and prancing, the chipmunks collide,
In a tangle of fur, they happily slide.
Giggles erupt as they tumble from view,
Falling like acorns, oh what a crew!

With floppy-eared bunnies and hats made of fluff,
They bounce through the branches, they can't get enough.
Cartwheels by owls, who are dizzy with joy,
In this topsy-turvy world, everyone's a toy.

And as the sun sets with the day's last embrace,
The giggles resound in the leafy space.
From high on their branches, they chortle and cheer,
For laughter and friendship are always so near!

Flight of Fancy

A squirrel takes off, with a whoosh and a zoom,
A joyride through branches, making them bloom.
Upside-down laughter, all around in a whirl,
As they acrobat tumble, giving fate a twirl.

A porcupine's slide, with a squeal and a laugh,
Tails in a tangle, creating quite the gaff.
Their antics and tricks bring the forest alive,
In this chaotic ballet, how we thrive!

With a chipper old crow acting as a judge,
Counting each stumble, not one can fudge.
With puns and homers, oh what a scene,
In this aerial circus, nonsense is keen.

As twilight descends, and the moon starts to rise,
The creatures all gather, bright stars in their eyes.
Sharing their tales of the day's merry chase,
In this fun-filled forest, there's always a place!

Laughter in the Leaves

Squirrels wear hats and dance all day,
Swinging from branches, they giggle away.
Acorns are tossed like popcorn high,
As birds chirp jokes that make us cry.

A raccoon dressed sharp, with a bright blue tie,
Tells tales of mischief as he scampers by.
The branches shake with the laughter's sound,
While leaves twirl around and tumble down.

A parrot squawks jokes that just won't quit,
While a tree frog leaps, landing with a split.
Nature's own circus, a riotous scene,
With every rustle a giggling machine.

From sunlit morn to the twilight's glow,
The canopy's stage puts on quite a show.
In this woodland gala, we join in the spree,
Where laughter's the language and fun flows free.

Dancing Among the Branches

In a shady grove where the sunlight prances,
Creatures all gather for impromptu dances.
Leaves rustle softly with a giggly cheer,
As a chipmunk does flips that bring us near.

A bear in a tutu shimmies with flair,
While an owl hoots softly without a care.
Together they whirl, a hilarious sight,
Under the moon's soft, silvery light.

The wind plays a tune on the whispering leaves,
While bumblebees buzz like the best of thieves.
They sway to the rhythm of nature's beat,
In this treetop bash that can't be beat.

With every rustle, a chuckle is found,
As critters join in, spinning round and round.
Amidst all the giggles, a lesson we've learned,
In dance and in laughter, our hearts have turned.

A Leap into the Unknown

A daring kangaroo takes a bold little jump,
Over a log with a thundering thump.
A squirrel watches wide-eyed with glee,
As branches quiver from enthusiasm's spree.

The ground rushes up, but he's light as a feather,
He lands with a bounce, like a spark in the weather.
Nearby, a wise tortoise shakes his head slow,
"Sometimes it's better to take things nice and low."

Through shrubs he hops, with a giggle and cheer,
His leaps making ripples of laughter appear.
The forest erupts in a cacophony bright,
As animals cheer for this daring delight.

So leap into moments that spark some delight,
Where joy is a landing, not a fearful fright.
With friends by your side, it's an adventure to roam,
In the great wild unknown, we'll always feel home.

The Treehouse Tales

In the treehouse high where the magic unfolds,
Stories are shared that the heart gently holds.
A raccoon starts off with a sly little grin,
As he pulls from the shelf a tale tucked within.

A pirate parrot with feathers all bright,
Tells tales of treasure under the moonlight.
The laughter erupts with each twist in the plot,
With giggles and gasps for adventures sought.

The wise old owl hoots a riddle so quirky,
While bunnies roll 'round, all hopped up and jerky.
Each tale spins a spark that ignites every dream,
As shadows dance softly and secrets all gleam.

At sunset, the treehouse becomes a grand stage,
Where critters perform, wild and outraged.
With stories of joy and a sprinkle of cheer,
These treehouse tales keep our laughter near.

Climbing Dreams

With giggles and gleeful shouts, we climb,
Branches sway, dancing with the time.
A squirrel drops acorns, oh what a mess,
The tree giggles back, what a funny jest!

Up we go, touching the sky,
Tangled in leaves that tickle and sigh.
A bird gives us looks, quite a surprise,
As we swing our legs with wide-open eyes.

From lofty heights, we spot a face,
A raccoon looks shocked in its own little space.
We wave and it waves, awkward and sweet,
In this battlefield of nature, we cannot be beat!

Falling down softly, like puffs of air,
This game of hide and seek, oh, we need to share!
Through laughter we tumble, through laughter we roar,
In this chase for joy, who could ask for more?

Breezy Boughs

Swinging from branches with a flappy cheer,
Trying to balance, whoops, lo and behold, here!
A raccoon on a limb, just chilling in style,
As we topple and giggle, he gives us a smile.

The winds whisper secrets, tickling our cheeks,
As we pull silly faces, not caring for peaks.
An owl hoots loudly, we think it's a cheer,
For the clumsy tree climbers, making their appear!

On leafy beds, we laugh till we cry,
Rolling down soft greens, wishing to fly.
With silly hats made from twigs and a grin,
We create our own world, where laughter begins.

In breezy boughs, we lose all our cares,
Embracing the silliness blown through our hairs.
In the midst of our laughter, we shout, "Hooray!"
For fun in the treetops, where we spend our day!

Shadows in the Sunlight

Underneath the branches, where shadows dance,
We do silly dances, giving joy a chance.
A bug with our rhythm, now that's a surprise,
As it jiggles along with its tiny sunrise.

With sunbeams chasing round the leafy green,
We perform our best antics, like a funny scene.
A parrot from above squawks, "You've got some style!"
We wink at our feathered friend, lending a smile.

Down comes a leaf, swaying as it falls,
Lands on our heads, oh the laughter calls!
We reach for the sun, stretch our limbs wide,
Creating our shadows, an amusing ride.

So under the sunlight, we twirl and spin,
With laughter and shadows, let the games begin!
In this quirky kingdom, the joy never ends,
With every absurd twist, our laughter ascends.

Embraces in the Heights

Up in the branches, reaching for fun,
We all hug in laughter, oh, it's a run!
A nest full of feathers holds giggles anew,
As we wobble and sway, the whole tree just flew!

The sun up above makes us squint with delight,
And fireflies join us, twinkling at night.
A friendly old crow gives a raucous caw,
While we tumble and roll without a single flaw.

Each embrace with a branch feels warm and alive,
As perching soon turns into a wobbly dive.
A whole world beneath is laughing along,
As we tumble and tumble, creating our song.

In the heights, together, we twist and we weave,
Finding friendships among leaves, which we never perceive.
With giggles and hugs, we soar wild and free,
In our leafy embrace, just you wait and see!

www.ingramcontent.com/pod-product-compliance
Lightning Source LLC
Chambersburg PA
CBHW051641160426
43209CB00004B/742